Draw an Easter scene below!

How many flowers can you count on this Easter egg?

There are 12 flowers.

Why shouldn't you tell an Easter egg a joke?

Because it might crack up!

Happy Easter

Circle the two bunnies that are the same.

ZZZ

How many cute critters can you count?

There are 12 critters.

Draw in the Easter bunny's ears. Add some eggs to the basket.

Decorate this Easter egg for the Easter bunny!